BATTLES OF SARATOGA

SARATOGA

A History from Beginning to End

Copyright © 2021 by Hourly History.

Table of Contents

Introduction

The Battles of Saratoga during the American War of Independence (also referred to as the American Revolution or the Revolutionary War) are commonly understood to be the turning point in that conflict when the British North American colonies truly began their march to victory against their colonial power, Great Britain. However, the history of these battles, their causes, and their impact are much more complicated than that.

The causes of the American Revolution itself are many and varied, and as historians have shown, they stretch back as far as the establishment of the North American colonies or even further. In order to understand the American Revolution, one must also understand its context. During the seventeenth and especially eighteenth centuries, a philosophical, scientific, political, and social movement known as the Enlightenment took place. At least in part as a result of the Enlightenment, several revolutions occurred in the ensuing century around the Atlantic World. The American Revolution was one of the first.

When the rebellion broke out, Great Britain did not expect the difficulty they would have in putting it down, but after the first battles in 1775 and as fighting dragged on into 1776, they began to question what these colonies were even worth. Meanwhile, the colonies issued the Declaration of Independence in July of 1776, greatly increasing fervor for independence at home.

The British tried many different military tactics to squash the uprising. The Battles of Saratoga were actually part of a larger campaign meant to cut off the northern colonies and New England. The British then planned to isolate the south, squash the fractured rebellion in the north, and reclaim control over their wayward colonies.

Saratoga is located along the Hudson River in New York. The Hudson River runs from New York City in the south all the way up into the Adirondack Mountains. It connects to other waterways, including the Mohawk River which runs northwest, and it was an enormously important thoroughfare in the eighteenth century. Saratoga is located on the river just north of Albany, the capital of New York. The Battles of Saratoga were a result of movements by the British to attempt to capture Albany.

The failure on the part of the British at Saratoga was a blow onto itself because it made the overall British strategy practically impossible.

But it was even more devastating for another reason: when King Louis XVI of France heard about the American victory at Saratoga, he finally decided to enter the war on the side of the Americans, which they had been lobbying for since before the first battles in 1775. All of a sudden, Britain's pesky colonial rebellion turned into a global war, one that threatened not only North America but also Britain's far more lucrative colonies in the Caribbean and around the world. That war continued beyond the British surrender at Yorktown in 1781.

It was largely for this reason that Britain chose to end the war in North America by granting the colonies the independence for which they had so desperately fought. Without the Battles of Saratoga, this may never have happened.

Chapter One

Colonial America: The Causes of the Revolutionary War

"Little strokes fell great oaks."

—Benjamin Franklin

In many ways, the seeds of revolution were planted as soon as Englishmen and Englishwomen stepped onto the shores of North America to establish new lives. The history of the British colonies that would one day form the original United States of America is long and complex. Therefore, this narrative will provide only a brief overview of this story, with special emphasis placed on the causes of the revolution as well as the history of New York, the colony in which the Battles of Saratoga took place.

The British first established North American colonies in two locations: at Jamestown, in what would become Virginia, located in the mid-Atlantic region, and at Plymouth in present-day Massachusetts, further north on the Atlantic coast. Both colonies were established in the first several decades of the seventeenth century, amid a frantic flurry by the great powers of Europe to expand territorially in the Americas.

The British North American colonies struggled at first but quickly began to flourish. They saw remarkable expansion and an explosion in population. After barely more than one hundred years, British citizens had established not only Massachusetts and Virginia, but Rhode Island, Pennsylvania, Connecticut, Maryland, New Hampshire, Delaware, New Jersey, North Carolina, South Carolina, and Georgia—twelve of the thirteen colonies that would rebel in the War of Independence. New York was originally a Dutch colony called New Amsterdam, which the British won in war in 1664.

There were several elements in most of the British colonies in North America that differentiated them from the colonies of France, Spain, and other European powers. One of the biggest and most relevant to understanding the revolution was the number of British subjects who settled in these colonies permanently. Unlike in many other places, they were not there to make their fortune and return to Great Britain. Instead, they purchased land, started farms or businesses, and established their lives in the New World. In large part, their children and future descendants also remained, creating a new generation of British subjects who had never even seen Great Britain itself. It was these younger generations that supported and fought in the Revolutionary War and established the United States of America.

The ways that the colonies were established and governed are also important to understanding the revolution. Each colony was established at different times and often for different reasons. Some were created through joint-stock companies, some by the British government itself, and still others were extensions of other colonies that eventually broke off. While Britain remained sovereign over all of them, most day-to-day operations were conducted at home, and these systems of governance varied greatly between the colonies. The lack of cohesiveness meant that a great deal of work went into uniting the colonies in the war against Great Britain and in the formation of the United States. That these two events occurred at all is in itself rather remarkable.

Colonization by the British (and all of Europe, for that matter) came at a steep price, particularly for the native peoples of North America. From the moment of contact with Europe, indigenous peoples of the Americas began dying in unprecedented numbers not only from warfare but also from disease. It is impossible to know the total death toll, but experts estimate that hundreds of millions of native people died as a direct result of contact with Europeans in what is the largest genocide in human history.

For those who survived, life was unimaginably altered. In some cases, the vast majorities of villages and even entire tribes were wiped out, causing a massive reorganization of people. Displacement was universal, and customs, religions, and age-old practices revolving around everything from farming to conversating were decimated. While the process of upheaval for the native peoples of North America continued for well over four hundred years from initial contact with Europe, an unimaginable amount of change also happened in the first few decades.

Relations with Native Americans contributed directly to the outbreak of the American War of

Independence. Warfare between the indigenous nations and the British colonists was practically constant. The reasons for this were many and complex, too complex for this narrative, but suffice it to say that the Europeans and their descendants were having difficulty respecting native claims to land. What was more, the British subjects believed that it was the duty of their government to protect them against the Native Americans. However, Indian wars were costly, in terms of both human life and money.

In an effort to both protect their citizens and maintain some semblance of peace, the British leadership entered into many agreements with the indigenous nations. These broke down for many reasons, not the least of which was that the colonists continually violated them by moving onto native land. During the American Revolution, many native leaders and their warriors fought alongside the British, believing that to be in their best interest. Once the United States achieved independence, the fate that they feared largely materialized. The Americans unleashed an unbridled avarice for land, displacing more and more native peoples and communities.

The founding of British North America also wrought unspeakable destruction across the Atlantic Ocean in Africa. The establishment of what would become the United States was largely dependent on slave labor, which would also prove to be a factor in why the southern colonies in particular rebelled in the 1770s (though slavery was legal in almost every corner of colonial North America, and many people were held in bondage in the north as well).

Partially due to some Enlightenment thinking, the practice of enslaving human beings was coming to be regarded as abhorrent by more and more people, and although Great Britain was still active in the trade in human lives, they also began to lean toward restriction and eventual abolition of slavery. The southern colonies in particular depended on slave labor to work their vast plantations growing tobacco, sugarcane, and cotton, which was quickly usurping all other crops as the most lucrative. What was more, many of these enslavers held a great deal of their wealth in human capital; their slaves were worth small fortunes on their own. The protection of their human investment was a major impetus for revolution for slave owners, who were among the wealthiest and most powerful people in the colonies (Thomas Jefferson, George Washington, James Madison, and many other Founding Fathers of America were themselves slave owners).

Thus, in some ways, the American Revolution was in part caused by the desire or need of the colonists to continue oppressing other peoples—both Africans and their descendants as well as native peoples. While the American Revolution espoused Enlightenment ideas in its rhetoric of equality and expansion of human rights, in practice, these benefits only applied to a small proportion of the American populace. It would take well over one hundred years for the young country to begin to expand these rights, and some would argue it still has a long way to go.

Another cause in the outbreak of the American Revolution was warfare in Europe, which frequently spilled over into the colonies. The most important conflict in regard to the causes of the American Revolution was undoubtedly the French and Indian War. It was actually part of the Seven Years' War fought in Europe between the British and French. While the British were victorious in this conflict, it was a long and brutal war that saddled all combatants with heavy debt.

At the same time, the American colonists had gained much from the Treaty of Paris, which ended the war. For one thing, the French were no longer a threat in most of North America, either militarily or economically, as competitors in the fur trade and other industries. For another, Great Britain greatly expanded its land holdings in North America, opening up much more land to the colonists. The British had even expelled French citizens from part of the territory they took.

In large part because they had gained so much from the war, the British government thought it was only fair that the colonies pay increased taxes in order to help pay for the costs. Thus begins the narrative of the causes of the American Revolution that American schoolchildren know so well: British Parliament taxed the colonists without awarding them representation in government, and the colonists balked at "taxation without representation." In reality, it was more complicated than that.

That said, the taxes levied in the wake of the French and Indian War fanned the flames of already growing anti-British sentiment in the thirteen North American colonies, and the colonial leadership, most of whom supported independence, used those taxes to stir up revolutionary fervor.

The first of these taxes was passed just two years after the signing of the Treaty of Paris which ended the French and Indian War. The Stamp Act of 1765 mandated that many paper products (everything from newspapers to playing cards) be printed on paper from London that bore a revenue stamp. It was designed to pay for the British soldiers stationed in the colonies to protect against attacks from both the French and Indians. The law was widely opposed by colonists even though it was meant to protect them.

Colonists flagrantly violated the act, and it prompted colonial leaders to hold the Stamp Act Congress (later referred to as the Continental Congress) in 1765. This was the first time that the colonies came together as a united front against the British government and was a major step in the coming of the revolution. They issued a Declaration of Rights and Grievances that was sent to Parliament and King George III. The king, as well as British leadership, were alarmed at these extralegal proceedings, but they repealed the Stamp Act nonetheless in order to avoid more conflict.

The victory on the part of the colonists was short-lived, however, because the Townshend Act was passed just two years later. The British government was in serious debt and demanded that their colonial subjects bear part of the burden. It is important to note that, especially at this point, not all (or even most) colonists favored independence. While they had no representation in Parliament, defenders of the British were keen to point out that the vast majority of British subjects in Great Britain were not landholders either and thus unable to vote, so they, too, were not privileged with direct representation.

The Townshend Act was actually a series of acts that placed duties or taxes on several products, such as glass, lead, paper, and most egregious, tea. Since these items had to be purchased from Great Britain, the colonists, in their growing free-market capitalist beliefs, balked at the mercantilist nature of them, and they were staunchly opposed with protests, boycotts, outright disobedience, and dissemination of anti-colonial and anti-British literature.

Things devolved pretty quickly from there. In 1770, British soldiers opened fire on a group of protestors in Boston, killing several colonists and wounding others. The event, which came to be called the Boston Massacre, was arguably one of the worst public relations events in history. It was widely publicized and propagandized by a group called the Sons of Liberty, among those leading the call for revolution and independence. Boston had been occupied by British soldiers for a couple of years at that point since it had been the location of so much unrest. Things only got worse within the city limits after this incident.

After the Boston Massacre, the British Parliament continued to pass and enforce taxes and duties on the colonies, one of the most despised being the Tea Act of 1773, which resulted in the famous Boston Tea Party, when the Sons of Liberty and their ilk dumped thousands of pounds worth of tea into the Boston Harbor. In response, the British effectively declared martial law in Boston, occupying not only the city itself but much of the colony of Massachusetts. They blockaded the harbor which caused serious economic hardship and terrified the people in Boston regarding possible famine or shortage of other supplies.

The leaders of the thirteen colonial governments met again the following year at the Continental Congress in Philadelphia. At this meeting, held from September 5 to October 26,

1774, twelve of the thirteen colonies (Georgia was not in attendance) agreed to give the king and Great Britain one more chance. They imposed heavy, unified boycotts on British goods to try to force their hand, as well. They were unsuccessful in getting Britain to relent to their demands, and less than a year later, the American Revolutionary War broke out.

Chapter Two

The American War of Independence

"Whenever any Form of Government becomes destructive of these ends, it is the Right of the People to alter or to abolish it, and to institute new Government."

—The Declaration of Independence

The actual beginning of the American War of Independence varies depending on who you ask since some colonies were in rebellion before others, and violence erupted between the colonists and the British military and government officials before 1775. However, historians generally agree that the war began in 1775; the colony of Massachusetts was declared to be in open rebellion by February, and the first battles of the war were fought in April.

As is clear from the previous chapter, tensions and even violence escalated for decades before the war began. However, the first shots were not fired until the Battles of Lexington and Concord on April 19, followed by the Battle of Bunker Hill on June 17 (all in Massachusetts). The Battle of Bunker Hill was a costly British victory, as more than one thousand soldiers were killed or injured when they were outnumbered by the American militia, a very high number for the eighteenth century, especially for what was still considered a rebellion. It showed the British that victory would not come easily, and that the rebellion may not be quick to quell. By the end of the summer of 1775, the rebellious colonists had shown how determined they were.

The colonists quickly turned their attention to Boston after the Battles of Lexington and Concord, with the goal of taking the city permanently from the British. For one thing, laying siege to Boston trapped several thousand British troops in the city, preventing them from reaching anywhere by land. For another, it would be a symbolic victory since the city of Boston was the site of so many important events leading to the revolution.

Meanwhile, leaders from all thirteen North American colonies were holding a series of meetings to decide on the best course of action.

They were also scrambling to establish interim governments and maintain order at home. They knew that if they could not protect lives and property, the populace would crave the control of the British government, and independence would be lost. As discussed in the previous chapter, the Continental Congress was held in 1774, and the leaders present at this meeting had already begun to lay the groundwork for these provisional governments and legislative bodies.

Especially compared to today, but even compared to one hundred years later, communication at this time was very slow. There were no railroads or steam-powered ships and no telegraph. Letters and information moved as slowly as people themselves. Therefore, it took a considerable amount of time to organize all thirteen colonies individually and collectively. Finally, by early July 1776, the colonies were ready to declare their independence from Great Britain.

That is exactly what they did on July 4, 1776, when representatives issued the Declaration of Independence. Penned by Thomas Jefferson but borrowing heavily from the Enlightenment works of John Locke (as well as other documents), it has become one of the most famous pieces of writing in American history. It explained, in both philosophical and practical terms, why the thirteen colonies were rebelling. Practically, they referenced the oppressive and unrepresentative government across the Atlantic. Philosophically, the Declaration of Independence cited universal human rights (which were at the time anything but universal) and the social contract between states and citizens.

With the signing of the Declaration of Independence, there could be no denying that the colonies were in rebellion, and both the British military and the colonies were busy preparing for more fighting. Most colonies had begun to raise support for independence and form militias to fight. Meanwhile, Britain was readying its military—arguably the most powerful in the world at the time—to crush this pesky uprising. At the same time, they had to preserve their more valuable Caribbean colonies.

The first major retaliation by the British was in the north, with a fight over the valuable port of New York in the New York and New Jersey Campaign. While the Battles of Saratoga also took place in the colony of New York, they were part of a separate campaign. The British were led by General William Howe, and the American colonial forces by General George Washington, a hero of the French and Indian War. While the American Continental Army had some successes, the campaign was largely a failure for them. They lost the Battle of Long Island (also called the Battle of Brooklyn), the largest battle in the entire war. What was more, the British maintained control of New York City, using it as a base and an important stronghold throughout the entire war. This was especially meaningful since Boston had fallen to the Americans.

By the end of the summer of 1776, General Washington had lost New York City. This loss was a major strategic blow to the Continental Army. Not only that, but it called Washington's leadership into question and gave many colonists who previously supported revolution pause. What if the colonies were not able to achieve independence, or even major concessions from Britain? Since they were in open rebellion, could that mean that citizens would be held guilty of treason for fighting or supporting the revolution? In addition, this achievement affirmed for the British that while the colonists scraped early victories, they would ultimately be unable to defeat one of the most powerful militaries in the world.

Nonetheless, Washington persevered. He and his troops fled across the Hudson River through New Jersey and all the way into Pennsylvania, and they did not arrive in good shape. Their numbers were greatly dwindled since the enlistment periods of many expired and others deserted what they now saw as a hopeless fight. But Washington wasn't beat yet, and his next move has become a treasured piece of American lore.

On December 25 to 26, 1776, Washington led his men by boat across the partially frozen Delaware River toward Trenton, New Jersey. This was a difficult feat this time of year and practically impossible without daylight. Nevertheless, somehow the men made it and were able to pull off a surprise attack that helped lead them to victory in the Battle of Trenton. For the beleaguered colonists who may have begun to lose faith in their ability to achieve independence, this was an immensely advantageous boost to morale.

The victory at the Battle of Trenton on December 26 was closely followed by another. Washington led his men to victory in the Battle of Princeton on January 3, 1777. It was also fought nearby Trenton in New Jersey. Washington and his men encamped in this region for the winter, very close to the British in New York City and Long Island. The two sides exchanged occasional fire in small skirmishes, but no more major battles occurred until the spring, as both armies focused on surviving the brutal winter.

By spring, the British were ready to retaliate and get revenge for what had transpired in the early winter. General Howe, who had already defeated Washington in New York, moved south in an attempt to capture the city of Philadelphia, the American capital at the time. With the rebels in control in Boston and the British in New York, capturing Philadelphia would strike a major blow. Unfortunately for Washington, Howe was successful. He defeated Washington in the Battle of Brandywine on September 11, 1777. Any attempts by the Americans to prevent him from marching into and occupying nearby Philadelphia just days later were also thwarted.

The capture of Philadelphia had, however, come at a steep price. General Howe received widespread criticism for the fact that he pursued this campaign instead of reinforcing General John Burgoyne's campaign further north. During his time in Philadelphia, Howe resigned from his post. His replacement, General Henry Clinton, would promptly begin withdrawing troops from Philadelphia to protect New York. In the next chapter, we will examine General Burgoyne's movements in northern New York and the campaign that resulted directly in the Battles of Saratoga.

Chapter Three

Prelude to the Battles at Saratoga

"Once vigorous measures appear to be the only means left of bringing the Americans to a due submission to the mother country, the colonies will submit."

—King George III

By this point in the war, the overall strategy of the British involved splitting the colonies, believing that if they isolated the south and north, the south would fall in line, and they could crush the fractured rebellion in the north. Further to that plan, they also schemed to divide New England itself, cutting off supply lines to both the military and civilians and forcing the populace to come to the conclusion that they had been better off under British rule. Taking control of eastern New York along the Hudson River, especially Albany, was key to that plan.

As part of this strategy, General John Burgoyne was directed to head south from the province of Quebec (in present-day Canada). The plan was that eventually, he would meet troops advancing from the south (New York City) and west (Ontario and western New York) and march into Albany in order to defeat the Americans there. Next, the plan was to capture the city, take control of the Hudson River, and completely isolate the New England colonies of the north from each other and from those in the mid-Atlantic and south.

It is important to keep in mind that even though all thirteen North American colonies signed the Declaration of Independence and agreed to fight toward that end, they were not all the same. The British government recognized the very pronounced differences between them, and as the war dragged on into its third year, they sought to exploit these differences. Believing the southern colonies to be more loyal than those in the north, the British thought that if they could isolate the colonies and the regions, they would start to drop out of the war one by one.

First, Burgoyne faced Fort Ticonderoga in the upper Hudson Valley region in early July of 1777. The Hudson River connects to other important bodies of water and was a major waterway used for trade and movement of troops. The British knew that access to this waterway would provide them with a crucial advantage. Fort Ticonderoga fell quickly and quietly, as Burgoyne's forces outnumbered the Americans by more than two-to-one. The British were able to occupy a strategically advantageous position early, causing the Americans to flee in the face of the superior numbers.

This was not only a military victory for the British but a moral victory as well. Americans were infuriated when they heard the fort was surrendered, including George Washington himself. It was very well fortified and important strategically. General Arthur St. Clair, who had been in charge at the fort, was removed from command along with his superior, General Philip Schuyler. Both were ruined by the loss.

Burgoyne's good luck would end there, though. He faced several setbacks over the next few weeks. For one thing, he had difficulty supplying his army and was stuck at Fort Edward (south of Fort Ticonderoga). Then, he found out that his counterpart to the west had to turn back after a bloody battle in which the British were defeated. This meant that the British would have far fewer men than planned when they reached Albany, jeopardizing the entire campaign. Finally, and most devastatingly, he suffered a major loss of his own on August 16. A force of well over two thousand colonial militiamen defeated his army, killing or capturing more than a thousand men at the Battle of Bennington in Vermont. Burgoyne began to grow more desperate, knowing he needed to find a safe place to encamp for the winter soon. Rather than turn back to Canada, he decided to proceed south to Albany. On his way, he would meet the Americans in the Battle of Saratoga.

Meanwhile, on the American side, General Schuyler had since been replaced with General Horatio Gates after the scandal involving Fort Ticonderoga. Gates enjoyed more support in the weeks leading up to the Battle of Saratoga than Burgoyne. Most importantly, Washington recognized the immense threat in the north and sent reinforcements. These reinforcements were not just more men; Washington sent some of his best strategists and lower-ranking commanders to meet Gates. One of these leaders was Benedict Arnold, who would eventually defect from the American to British side later in the war.

Gates marched north in early September. When he arrived north of Albany, he set up defenses at a location called Bemis Heights, about ten miles south of the town of Saratoga. He chose this strategic location because it provided a clear view of the area for miles around. It also allowed him to see the Hudson River and the only road leading to Albany.

However, it was not all smooth sailing for Gates. He was embroiled in a major feud with one of his top-ranking officers, Benedict Arnold. The two had never gotten along, but the situation worsened in the weeks leading up to the Battle of Saratoga. During the battle, their inability to work together or even communicate would cost more than a few soldiers their lives. It also contributed to Arnold's eventual betrayal and defection to the British.

Meanwhile, fresh off his loss at the Battle of Bennington, Burgoyne was headed south once again. He wound up encamping a few miles from the Americans, just north of Saratoga. As he did so, skirmishes broke out periodically in minor encounters between soldiers, and both sides knew that the battle was imminent.

In addition to his other woes, Burgoyne was at another disadvantage at this point; most of the

Native American warriors who supported him had abandoned not only him but the British as a whole, especially after the loss at the Battle of Bennington. Many indigenous nations allied with the British at the outbreak of the war, but they were quickly dropping out or even changing sides.

It is important to understand this strategy not so much as one of affinity but of survival. Knowing that westward movement and the acquisition of more land was a cause of the war in the first place, many Indians feared what would happen to them if the colonists were put in charge. When they looked at the situation objectively, they saw that the British had been a mitigating force that held the colonies back from further decimating their nations. They believed that if they had to accept Europeans in their homeland, they were better off under British rule than American.

As the war progressed, though, and the British lost more and more battles, some leaders of indigenous tribes and nations began to reconsider. Most of all, they likely feared their fates in the event of an American victory—could they be hanged for treason? Especially in regions where the British were losing, like northern New York and Vermont, they were also losing support among the Native Americans. Now, they were isolated and surrounded in upstate New York. The Battle of Saratoga was about to begin.

Chapter Four

First Battle: The Battle of Freeman's Farm

"We should never despair; our Situation before has been unpromising and has changed for the better, so I trust, it will again."

—George Washington

The Battle of Freeman's Farm took place on September 19, 1777. As battles sometimes did in the eighteenth century, this one began by accident, even though its eventual outbreak was imminent. Arnold strongly suspected that the British would try to flank the Americans from the American left position and tried to convince Gates of this, but their rivalry stood in the way of Gates listening to him. Arnold finally received approval to send out some of his troops in that direction early in the morning of the battle on a reconnaissance mission. They found what they were looking for, proving Arnold right: British advance soldiers moving toward the line. The first shots were fired in a nearby field belonging to a man named John Freeman (hence the name of this battle).

The sound of gunfire quickly alerted both sides that something was amiss. One of the leaders of the reconnaissance mission, Daniel Morgan, acted swiftly. He directed his marksmen into strategic positions, and they shot and killed many of the officers in the British advance unit. Then, he charged at the remaining soldiers. Morgan's marksmen would be crucial to the Americans in this battle, causing a great deal of problems for the British.

Initially, Morgan and his men believed that they had been successful in their maneuvers. However, at the time they did not know that the men they encountered were not on their own; they were, in fact, an advance guard, and most of the British soldiers in the region were headed directly for them. In the meantime, other men had raced back to the American encampment to alert Gates to what happened, and he and his leadership readied the rest of their men for battle.

The fighting continued in and around the field, as the British troops marched further toward the Americans and the Americans scrambled into formation. Throughout the day, the battle unfolded in spurts, alternating between periods of intense fighting and eerie quiet. Both sides revealed their advantages in this battle, which would come into play again when the second Battle of Saratoga occurred. The Americans had some expert marksmen in their ranks, Morgan's men chief among them. They camouflaged themselves in trees and in densely wooded areas in order to target British artillery operators and officers. Undoubtedly, they had learned this from fighting with and against indigenous warriors, who had been using guerilla tactics in warfare for centuries. The British, on the other hand, were much better at both cavalry and infantry charges and holding their lines in formation, especially when the fighting became intense. After all, this was the style that they were used to fighting in Europe, and the British were well-known for their disciplined ranks.

The fighting continued in a back-and-forth style in this way for several hours. In the early evening around 5 pm, General Burgoyne ordered Baron Friedrich Adolf Riedesel, a German officer leading a Hessian force fighting for the British, to charge the American right flank. The offensive paid off; by the time night had fallen, the British not only held the field but had also protected their vital supply lines. The Americans were forced back behind their fortifications into their camp.

Mostly because they were the ones standing on the field at the end of the day, the British were declared victorious in the First Battle of Saratoga, but it had cost them dearly. Burgoyne suffered around six hundred casualties, which was a huge number for the time, especially in a colonial war. While the Continental Army had lost ground, they only had about half the number of dead and wounded as the British.

Remember, the overall British goal was to take Albany and divide the Continental Army and the Americans in general in the north. Then, the British could initiate a strategy of divide and conquer and end the rebellion quickly. The victory at Freeman's Farm was an important step in the right direction, but it was a small one and had cost them dearly. They had gained ground, but not a lot, since the Americans were still encamped in the same place and had lost far fewer soldiers.

The stage was set for fighting to break out again, and it did, less than three weeks later. Before examining that battle, however, it is important to take a look at what happened on both sides in between the two engagements.

Chapter Five

Between the Battles

"Objects of the most stupendous magnitude, and measure in which the lives and liberties of millions yet unborn are intimately interested, are now before us. We are in the very midst of a revolution the most complete, unexpected, and remarkable of any in the history of nations."

—John Adams

While the Battles of Saratoga are frequently treated as a singular event (often even referred to as simply the Battle of Saratoga), nearly three weeks passed between the two major engagements. During those eighteen days, both armies made crucial decisions and took actions that impacted the outcome of the second battle and the war itself.

General Burgoyne strongly considered attacking the Americans again the very next day. They had been forced to retreat and were in a weakened position. However, he decided against it for a couple of reasons. The first was logistical. His own men were tired and weak, and many were not still standing; remember, his numbers were drastically impacted by the losses on September 19. They needed time not only to rest and recuperate but to replace damaged equipment and get prepared. Ideally, they also needed reinforcements. That process would take longer than twelve hours.

The other reason was strategic. Burgoyne received news that General Henry Clinton, who was garrisoned in New York City, would have by then been making his way up the Hudson River toward Burgoyne. Desperately in need of supplies and reinforcements, Burgoyne bet that if he could be joined by Clinton, the combined forces would easily defeat the Americans, end the fighting north of Albany, and that the city would fall quickly thereafter, with few troops left in the region to defend it. Therefore, he began to strategize how to postpone another major engagement before Clinton and his men reached the region.

So, instead of attacking right away when the Americans were the weakest, Burgoyne waited. In the immediate aftermath, the British soldiers tended to the wounded, buried the dead, and recovered from the intense battle. He wrote to General Clinton, explaining the precarious situation in which he and his troops found themselves, and asked for help. Then, he worked to strengthen his own lines and defenses.

Things were not peaceful in the American camp. The disappointment over losing ground after such a hard day of fighting escalated into a shouting match among leadership. The rivalry between Horatio Gates and Benedict Arnold has already been mentioned, and when Gates wrote his report of the battle, he scarcely mentioned Arnold, even though Arnold had been on the field all day and commanded some of the most important maneuvers. Arnold exploded in anger, and he had the support of many of his men behind him. Gates dismissed Arnold from his post and granted him a transfer to Washington's command, though Arnold chose to remain with his men in New York.

Meanwhile, much was happening nearby that, while unbeknownst to the combatants in Saratoga at the time, would in some ways impact the outcome of the second battle. For one thing, Clinton had moved north from New York City, though later than he originally planned. He sailed up the Hudson River and engaged the Americans in the Battles of Fort Clinton and Fort Montgomery, just a few miles south of West Point. He was victorious, dealing a blow to the Americans. West Point was an important locale as it was the western point of the Hudson River. Over the course of the following year, Americans built fortifications there to replace the lost forts, and it became the site of the United States Military Academy, which is still in service today.

The Americans also launched offensives in the time between the two battles. They attempted to re-take Fort Ticonderoga but were not successful. This is hardly surprising given how well constructed and defended that fort was, which was part of the reason so many were angry when the Americans lost it in the first place. That said, they were successful in smaller engagements around the fort. The forces there swelled when units in various parts of the region joined each other. They took smaller forts, encampments, and territory as far south as Lake George, which is located a few miles north of Saratoga. Crucially, they then joined the Americans, swelling their ranks by about 2,000 men.

As the time between the battles went on, the Americans also enjoyed strong supply lines, which meant that they not only had plenty of food and other survival items (such as bandages, blankets, and clothing) but a lot of ammunition as well. More and more, as time went on, they became better prepared for the next battle.

It was not completely quiet between the British and Americans in Saratoga, either. Daily, small skirmishes broke out, mostly between men on patrols. The marksmen on the American side who were so familiar with Indian warfare continued to harass the British, picking off men unexpectedly, making any movement, foraging, or scouting very dangerous for the British. To make matters even worse for the British, they were plagued by desertions, which increased after October 3, when food was rationed because of dwindling supplies. When captured by the Americans, these men divulged information about the situation in the British camp, swelling the Americans' confidence.

As time went on, things on the British side became more desperate, in contrast to the Americans, who received a morale boost at the arrival of the men under the command of General Benjamin Lincoln from the north. It became clear to Burgoyne by early October that Clinton was not coming to reinforce the British at Saratoga, and Burgoyne despaired over how he could possibly be successful at taking the region and marching on Albany. He even convened meetings with other officers under his command. Several of them, including Riedesel, favored retreating, but Burgoyne insisted on pursuing the offensive. Therefore, they agreed that on the morning of October 7, they would attack the Americans at their left flank. What they did not know was the renewed strength of the army they were about to face.

Chapter Six

Second Battle: The Battle of Bemis Heights

"While we remember that we are contending against brothers and fellow subjects, we must also remember that we are contending in this crisis for the fate of the British Empire."

—John Burgoyne

The Battle of Bemis Heights took place on October 7, 1777. As stated in the last chapter, Burgoyne did not want to leave Saratoga and retreat, as had been suggested by some of his other officers. So, during the morning hours, he and some of his top officers went on a reconnaissance mission to the American left flank. Because they employed a large number of troops to accompany and protect them, they were impossible to miss. Once the Americans spotted them and word got back to General Gates, he ordered Morgan and his sharpshooters into the fray to take strategic aim at anyone they could, officers being the primary target.

Gates did not stop with the marksmen, though. Assuming this was the second battle that they had been anticipating, he ordered other units and regiments into formation as well. He took command of the left flank (where the strike was anticipated), and since he had dismissed Benedict Arnold, he gave General Lincoln, who had arrived with reinforcements since the Battle of Freeman's Farm, command of the right. In all, more than 6,000 men assembled for battle during the late hours of the morning on October 7.

Once again, the coming battle erupted not as the result of a carefully planned offensive, but by happenstance. Burgoyne's reconnaissance mission was spotted, and the Americans responded by preparing for battle. Therefore, it was not until a couple hours into the afternoon that the fighting actually began. Fighting broke out around 2 pm. The first phase of the battle was not good for the British. Along the American left flank, Morgan and his marksmen were at work, helping the other Americans in the region overcome a numerical disadvantage and prevent British forces from moving west. Burgoyne himself was almost killed, narrowly escaping disaster. After the arrival of more American reinforcements under the command of Brigadier General Abraham Ten Broeck, the British on the left flank were forced to retreat.

Meanwhile, closer to the American center, Brigadier General Enoch Poor ordered his militiamen to hold fire and hold their positions a distance away from the British. This forced Major Acland and his British grenadiers to advance and eventually engage in a bayonet charge. At that point, Poor's men opened fire on the charging grenadiers, inflicting massive casualties. The Americans were able to take Acland, who had been injured, and several of his high-ranking officers prisoner, as well as capturing their artillery.

Within barely an hour, these two movements had eliminated around 400 British troops, through death, injury, or capture, not to mention the seizure of so much heavy artillery. Gates then decided to do what Burgoyne had failed to do after the first battle: he struck back while the British were at their weakest.

Up until this point in the day, Benedict Arnold had remained in his camp, having been dismissed from Gates' service. Now, he emerged for the second half of the day. The circumstances under which he chose to do so are not well-established in the historical record, which adds to the intrigue surrounding his eventual defection. Whether or not he had Gates' permission, he rode into battle (possibly drunk) and helped lead the chase.

As the British fled, they headed in the direction of a redoubt (a temporary, square fortification without flanking) commanded by Hessian Lieutenant Colonel Heinrich von Breymann and General Alexander Lindsay. As the troops approached the defenses, incredibly fierce fighting broke out, largely led by Arnold, whose vigor renewed the frightened and wearied American troops. He led two dangerous charges through weaknesses in the redoubt, and was supported by Morgan's sharpshooters, who had gone around to attack from the rear. Many lives were lost, especially British lives, and von Breymann himself was also killed.

After several narrow escapes, Benedict Arnold was also injured. After his horse was shot, he was shot in the leg at the same time that his horse fell on that same leg, crushing it. He was carried back to the camp, and the broken leg has become somewhat legendary. A monument featuring a model of Arnold's boot still stands on the battlefield today. The injury in large part ended Arnold's military career.

The fighting on October 7 only ended because of nightfall, which was incredibly fortunate for the British, since their camp was now exposed to the Americans after they broke through the redoubt. The Americans retreated back into their camp for the night. That said, it was not a given that fighting would not resume the next day, and the Americans began to prepare accordingly. Meanwhile, Burgoyne commenced a retreat to the north.

By the end of both battles, the British had lost around one thousand men, almost twice the number of American casualties. Among the dead were several important officers, and they had also lost a sizeable amount of artillery, horses, and other vital supplies. General Burgoyne finally surrendered to General Gates on October 17, though he had known for days—with his army outnumbered and surrounded—that he had lost. According to customs dictating "civilized" warfare at the time, Burgoyne and his remaining men were allowed to march to Boston, under pretenses of sailing back to Europe (remember, the Americans held Boston). The Americans in Boston held them captive until the end of the war.

Chapter Seven

Aftermath

"The times that tried men's souls are over—and the greatest and completest revolution the world ever knew, gloriously and happily accomplished."

—Thomas Paine

Once again, the Battles of Saratoga are regarded as the turning point in the American Revolution, and in many ways, they were. One of the biggest impacts of the battles was the entry of the French into the war. National histories of the revolution hold that after the American victories at Saratoga, the French realized that it was a winnable fight and were finally convinced to support the fledgling nation. It is well-established that when the king of France, Louis XVI, received word of the resounding victory, he was convinced to throw his support behind the rebellious colonies.

In many ways, this was a controversial decision. In retrospect, we now see the Americans as a fledgling nation, but at the time, that was not a given. The American War of Independence was not a conflict between two enemy combatant states; technically, it was an internal rebellion. At least in the recent past of the time, it was not typical for foreign powers, especially enemies, to intervene in these situations. But the Americans had been sending communication and envoys to France for many months to try to convince them that theirs was a cause worth supporting.

Events in Europe and around the world also influenced France's decision to aid the Americans. Perhaps more than anything, the Battles of Saratoga confirmed for the French that the revolution would be a long and costly war for the British, and the financial and military distraction was something the French could exploit to their own advantage. With the entry of the French into the war, it truly became a global conflict, threatening not only the British colonies in North America but the Caribbean and the rest of the world, as well. This would be a major factor in Britain's decision to end the war and grant American independence.

However, neither the British nor the Americans marched onto great triumph in the north after the Battles of Saratoga. Instead, a stalemate ensued. The French Navy assisted in

Rhode Island but decided that an attack on New York, the British stronghold, was too risky. The Americans enjoyed other victories, but the winter of 1779/1780, when Washington and his men were encamped at Valley Forge, dealt them a serious blow. This winter was especially brutal, and the army experienced hunger, disease, and desertions.

Many of the important battles during the rest of the war took place in the southern colonies. In fact, the Americans and the French dealt the British their final blow in the Yorktown Campaign and at the Battle of Yorktown, fought in the early fall of 1781. It was after this engagement that General Cornwallis, the commander of British forces in North America, surrendered to George Washington. And thus began the saga of American nationhood.

Of course, the end of the American Revolution was much more complex than a military victory on the part of the colonies. The British chose to surrender for many reasons separate from the military prowess of their North American rebels. What was more, the British planned to re-take the colonies eventually and did not see the end of the war as the end of their influence in the region. Land was constantly changing hands during this time all around the world, so this was not at all an unreasonable assumption. And indeed, they were nearly successful in the War of 1812, often regarded by modern historians as the second war for American independence.

After the Battles of Saratoga, General Burgoyne was recalled to Great Britain, and while he remained in the military, he was never again given command. His reputation never recovered from this loss, despite the fact that many of the conditions that contributed to his defeat were out of his control. That said, the argument can certainly be made that, had Burgoyne attacked the Americans on the day after the Battle of Freeman's Farm, he may have been victorious. After all, the Americans received crucial reinforcements of both soldiers and supplies in the days that intervened between the two engagements. Or, as others have argued, had Burgoyne retreated and then met the Americans on another front, with reinforcements and different leadership, the outcome could also have been very different. Regardless of whether General Burgoyne could have made different decisions, though, he lived the rest of his life in ignominy.

On the American side, General Gates had a rather interesting experience throughout the rest of the war. First, he was part of a plan to replace George Washington as commander in chief that failed during late 1777 and early 1778, after the Battles of Saratoga. He was also later blamed for the defeat at the Battle of Camden in New Jersey on August 16, 1780. His military reputation decimated, he did not command again during the war, but after the war, he freed his slaves, moved to New York, and served a term in the state legislature.

Of course, Benedict Arnold's actions during the rest of the war are the stuff of legend. He infamously turned spy for the British and eventually made a formal defection to their side. After believing himself passed over for several promotions and marrying into a wealthy Loyalist family, Arnold planned to hand West Point to the British and fled to their side in 1780 after his plot was discovered.

In many ways, Arnold paid for his betrayal for the rest of his life. He was vilified by Americans, who used his name as an insult or expletive for decades after the war was over. He moved to London before the war even ended. Even while there, he encountered a great deal of hatred, particularly from political opponents and other army retirees. He attempted to leave Britain and join his sons in Canada but again faced such disrespect that he decided he had been better off in London and returned, where he lived out the remainder of his 60 years of life. His bravery during the Battles of Saratoga has done little to redeem him in the annals of American history.

The Battles of Saratoga not only had an indelible impact on the rest of the war (particularly the outcome) but on those who fought in it as well. It has continued to be taught, remembered, and even celebrated in the United States.

Chapter Eight

Legacy

"The Constitution of the United States was made not merely for the generation that then existed, but for posterity—unlimited, undefined, endless, perpetual posterity."

—Henry Clay

The Battles of Saratoga are well-remembered today. Much of that is not only attributed to their importance but to the efforts of Americans themselves. The first few generations after the war, however, were not as interested in preservation as later generations. During the late eighteenth century and at least the first half of the nineteenth, Americans were more forward-looking and concerned with progress than with preserving the past. It wouldn't be for more than one hundred years after the battle until the preservation movement began in the late nineteenth century. At that time, Americans and people in other countries (typically western countries) experienced a surge of interest in the past. There were several reasons for this, including a cultural revival of colonial architecture, art, and design.

The Sons of the American Revolution and the Daughters of the American Revolution were founded in 1889 and 1890, respectively. Americans were in the middle of celebrating the centennial of the revolution, the founding of their nation, and many other monumental events. The years-long centennial was especially important because it was celebrated by the first generation of Americans after the bloody, brutal American Civil War. It was during this coming together and long celebration of the past that Americans began to look at the history all around them. This included battlefields.

The land on which the Battles of Saratoga were fought came under the jurisdiction of New York State and its preservation efforts in 1927, on the 150th anniversary of the battles. Eleven years later, the United States Congress authorized the creation of the Saratoga National Historic Parks under the National Park System, as the government scrambled to create jobs during the Great Depression. From there, park officials have worked diligently to preserve the terrain and maintain the overall look (mostly by controlling tree and grass growth), explore the natural surroundings, and uncover artifacts. In addition, they preserve the physical manmade structures on the battlefield and nearby, like General Philip Schuyler's home.

In addition to preservation efforts of the battlefield itself, the Battles of Saratoga are considered a major event in the history of the United States. As such, they are taught to schoolchildren at several points in their history education, and many adults can describe (in broad strokes) what it was and why it was important. All of this attests to the long-recognized importance of the battle, which historians have been unable to refute. Unless an entirely new interpretation emerges from the historical annals, it is unlikely the Battles of Saratoga will decline in historical importance.

Though no historians wholly deny the importance of the Battles of Saratoga, that does not mean that there are not aspects of it that are still up for debate. There is an ongoing debate among historians about who the victory at the Battle of Saratoga is to be chiefly attributed. Gates famously claimed credit in the years afterward, as he was the commanding officer. But some historians also point to blunders on the part of the British, General Lincoln, and most controversially, Benedict Arnold. Both Arnold and Gates produced records during their lifetimes that emphasized their own roles in the battles.

The Battles of Saratoga have also been understood in different ways and under different historical interpretations. Interestingly, many more recent transnational historians have established connections between revolutions around the world, particularly around the Atlantic Ocean. Certainly, the American Revolution contributed to revolutionary fervor elsewhere, including France and France's Caribbean colony of Haiti. Not only did the Battles of Saratoga help draw the French into the fight, but they also helped establish the very idea that colonial entities could successfully rise up and defeat some of the most powerful militaries in the world.

Regardless of which historian you consult or what historical perspective you take, the Battles of Saratoga—particularly the American victory at Bemis Heights—remain one of the most decisive events in the American Revolution and in colonial history.

Conclusion

Fought in September and October of 1777, the Battles of Saratoga were truly the turning point of the American Revolution. They defeated the overall strategic plan of the British at the time—to divide and conquer the colonies. They prevented the British from taking control of Albany and the Hudson River. And they convinced the French to enter the war on the American side, turning a colonial revolution into a global war.

The importance of the Battles of Saratoga has been emphasized throughout the narrative. Had the Americans not been victorious in the Battles of Saratoga, it is possible that the war may have dragged on far longer, causing untold further damage and loss of life. Or perhaps the Americans may not have been victorious at all in the quest for independence. Obviously, it is impossible to know. What is well-established fact is the monumental impact of the Battles of Saratoga in the formation of the United States of America.

Bibliography

Chernow, R. (2007). *Washington: A Life.*

Ferling, J. (2007). *Almost a Miracle: The American Victory in the War of Independence.*

Ketchum, R.M. (1999). *Saratoga: Turning Point of America's Revolutionary War.*

Lengel, E.G. (2020). *The Ten Key Campaigns of the American Revolution.*

Library of Congress, The. "The American Revolution, 1763-1783." https://www.loc.gov/classroom-materials/united-states-history-primary-source-timeline/american-revolution-1763-1783/

Museum of the American Revolution Online. https://www.amrevmuseum.org/

National Park Service. Saratoga National Historic Park. https://www.nps.gov/sara/index.htm

Philbrick, N. (2014). *Valiant Ambition: George Washington, Benedict Arnold, and the Fate of the American Revolution.*

Snow, D. (2016). *1777: Tipping Point at Saratoga.*

Wood, G.S. (2003). *The American Revolution: A History.*

Made in United States
North Haven, CT
21 December 2023

46436798R00036